GW01071889

The Devil's Bookshop

DAVID KENNEDY was born in Leicester in 1959. He co-edited *The New Poetry* and is the author of *New Relations: The Refashioning of British Poetry 1980–1994*. He edits *The Paper*, a magazine of innovative poetry and poetics, and publishes widely on contemporary poetry in English. His publications include *The President of Earth: New and Selected Poems*; *The Dice Cup*, translations of Max Jacob's prose poems with Christopher Pilling; *Cornell: A Circuition Around His Circumambulation*; the collaboration *Eight Excursions* with Rupert Loydell; and *The Roads*. David lives in Sheffield with his wife Christine.

Also by David Kennedy

Poetry
>The Roads (Salt, 2004)
>Eight Excursions collaboration with Rupert Loydell (The Cherry On The Top Press, 2003)
>The President of Earth: New and Selected Poems (Salt, 2002)
>Cornell: A Circuition Around His Circumambulation (West House Books, 2001)
>Max Jacob: The Dice Cup Part I translation with Christopher Pilling (Atlas, 2000)
>The Elephant's Typewriter (Scratch, 1996)

Books about Poetry
>Elegy (Routledge, 2007)
>Douglas Dunn (Northcote House/Writers and Their Work, 2007)
>New Relations: The Refashioning of British Poetry 1980–1994 (Seren, 1996)

As Editor
>Necessary Steps: Essays on Poetry, Elegy, Walking, Spirit (Shearsman, 2007)
>Additional Apparitions: Poetry, Performance & Site Specificity with Keith Tuma (The Cherry On The Top Press, 2002)
>The New Poetry with Michael Hulse and David Morley (Bloodaxe Books, 1993)

The Devil's Bookshop

DAVID KENNEDY

SALT

CAMBRIDGE

PUBLISHED BY SALT PUBLISHING
PO Box 937, Great Wilbraham, Cambridge PDO CB1 5JX United Kingdom

© David Kennedy, 2007

The right of David Kennedy to be identified as the
author of this work has been asserted by him in accordance
with Section 77 of the Copyright, Designs and Patents Act 1988.

Salt Publishing 2007

Printed and bound in the United Kingdom by Biddles Ltd

Typeset in Swift 9.5 / 13

ISBN 978 1 84471 317 2 hardback

Salt Publishing Ltd gratefully acknowledges
the financial assistance of Arts Council England

1 3 5 7 9 8 6 4 2

To Christine, who makes everything possible

Contents

Acknowledgements

'The Bombs, July 2005', 'Calendar', 'for Cage: Changes / Pages', 'The Lost Room', 'The Metamorphosis of Gaëtan Dugas', 'Near Death', 'The Waters' and 'Winter Windows' were written as part of an AHRC Fellowship in Creative & Performing Arts 2004–2007 hosted by English in the Department of Humanities at Leeds Trinity & All Saints. Special thanks are due to Head of Humanities, Joyce Simpson, and to my mentor Oz Hardwick.

'Calendar' and 'Near Death' were first published in *Fulcrum*.

'The Bombs, July 2005' and 'The Waters' were first published as sound files on *The Archive of the Now* website directed by Andrea Brady and hosted by Brunel University.

An earlier version of 'Winter Windows' appeared in my practice based essay 'Mourning After: Writing Elegies in the 21st Century', accessible on the British Electronic Poetry Centre website. An e-mail from Stephen Vincent provided the quoted sentence that begins the version published here.

'Three Postscripts' was also first published as part of 'Mourning After: Writing Elegies in the 21st Century'.

'Prospectus' was first published in *Hard Times* nr. 80 as 'The Weather in the Mountains'.

Guy Babineau's article 'The Prettiest One: Remembering Gaëtan Dugas' provided the details of Dugas's physical appearance and the story of the cherry tree that appear in the elegy that opens this collection. The article is available at: http://members.shaw.ca/guy babineau/patientzero.htm. Professor George Kinghorn directed me to factual sources for HIV/AIDS not wrapped up in politics or stigma that also proved invaluable in researching the poem.

The quotation 'It's a mirror, you provide the formula' in 'Entry on Nation' is from Steven Soderburgh's film *Solaris* (2002).

Joanna Boulter, Peter Riley and Jonathan Styles helped with the definition of *musica ficta*.

Patrick McGuinness helped with the antique meanings of 'boucaner' in 'The Devil's Bookshop'. Jacques Terrasson came up with the phrase 'J'aime mieux boucaner que bouquiner' that set the piece in motion; and Jean Markale taught me that the first books came from 'boucs'.

The Metamorphosis of Gaëtan Dugas

Gaëtan Dugas (20.02.53–30.03.84), erroneously identified as 'Patient Zero'
and wrongly held responsible for spreading AIDS in America.

The words of the world keep buzzing, swarming,
painting black any sun that warmed you.
No wonder it feels so late and it is
but not so dark your blond hair and green eyes
can't be made out quite clearly as a man's
not a beast's feasting on its monstrous lust;
your Beach Boy Jesus beauty as beauty,
unqualified, purely its own reason.

And I must start with your body,
site of all the bother,
otherwise I'm copying a ghost
made by others. Your afterlife's
a half-life: your printed voice
showers death, makes desire a wand
forever striking forth shapes transformed
and bodies strange; you're spread from site

to site to site like, yes, a virus.
So I must remember your body,
your good body and wonderful skin.
Then I must call you 'brother'
because naming you zero makes you
a hole, a dirty sink, a poisoned outlet,
more and less than yourself, an origin
and nothing, the lowest and the first,

a vanishing point risen above the horizon.
You've been a tale from Ovid long enough,
a one-way system of loss and rupture.
Beautiful metamorph, come back to yourself
from the demon lover, folkloric black hat

of a biotic drama. Show us again
the fivefold form of your feet and hands,
your ridgeless forehead, your smooth temples.

You won't know Vancouver's city fathers said 'yes'
then quickly 'no' to a cherry tree for you
in Stanley Park. Your pink petals
might lead to others, crash the ecosystem.
They grudged your friends some shore, a wedge
between the park and a hotel. Even in death
you're only allowed to be a space,
a disuse the four winds can chafe.

Last I read the tree's pulled through, untended.
It stands, exchanging earth and the heavens
that spangle the Strait of Georgia's watery floor.
Perhaps a Pisces *should* be called to mind by water
but you're owed much larger recompense
than this unnoticed, trembling marker.
My song alone can't bring you in
from the raw weather of exception,

and the words swarming, and back inside the walls.
All these lines have in their gift
is arguing for an archaeology
with which we tag the words your tongue made
and you become again the author of your acts.
Life goes on where the streets begin:
through them runs the profit of the dead
—not what they leave but how we spend their loss.

The Bombs, July 2005

Trying to join words
to four bombs,

words that are not,
words that are not,

words that are not,
that are not,

are not
like carnage,

atrocity, screens
around the bombs.

Or trying to join words
to four men,

words that are not,
like jihad, cell,

screens
around the men.

Or trying to start
from the same point:

how much
they hated

us: our fierce,
pointless individualisms.

Trying to join words
to four bombs,

to four men,
words that are not,

trying I stood up
in a room

nine days later,
before a reading,

and said something
about a line

with 'harm' at one end
and, at the other,

'care' where
poetry is

showing us care.
I stood up

trying to join words
that would stand.

Standing,
I tried to word joins.

Balanced
on the tip

of trying,
I tried to join words,

words that won't
make the living

or the dead cringe
and crawl away

and turn their faces
to the wall.

[4]

Calendar
after Spenser's The Shepheardes Calendar *(1579)*

Jan and Feb are idylls,
but plaintive, winterbeaten.
The mails clogged with poems
yearning for publishers.
With distant shepherds competing with each other.
    And where are the dead?
    Not resting, not gone.
    Not withered in the cold earth.
Our heads are hotels
where we teach the dead how to live.
How to watch the days go by.
When to appear.
Which dreams to inhabit.
What, if anything, to say in them.

March and April are darts
of beautiful regard.
Wounding stick figures
out on to catwalks.
Spearing the annual tribute.
    And where are the dead?
    Not gone, not resting,
    not withered in the cold earth.
Our eyes are projectors
screening the dead.
This half minute, that ten seconds.
Slower and slower.
On wider and wider screens.
Watching each nuance assemble, decompose.

May and June are songs,
ringing clear in mazy thickets.
Between the branches,
the sun flashes
off the crystal floor of heaven.
    And where are the dead?
    Not resting, not gone.
    Not withered in the cold earth.
Our bones are scaffolding
round listed buildings.
Behind plastic's clatter and flap
we strip off usage, bring back
what we never possessed.
The paradox of fidelity.

July and August are
delectable controversies
whose dialect differs from the common.
Cathedral noons; at night, the same domes
crossed by comets and blazing stars.
    And where are the dead?
    Not resting, not gone.
    Not withered in the cold earth.
Our tongues are jetties,
runways, platforms, hard landings,
where the dead itch to step down
or step off; obedient to the story.
Its exemplary situations.
Our doubts about it.

September and October.
Lugubrious seasons of the bass clarinet.
Winding dapper ditties
into unnatural rages
around the cogs and escapements of weather.
  And where are the dead?
  Not resting, not gone.
  Not withered in the cold earth.
Our skin is an archive.
Shared or multiple authorings
of anonymous or particular ecstasies.
An archive producing a past.
A past being constantly changed.
The fidelity of paradox.

November and December.
Delights laid abed
and welkin curdled.
Cupid shivering in a bare thicket.
At his back, a quiver of cold iron.
  And where are the dead?
  Not resting, not gone.
  Not withered in the cold earth.
Our bodies are reservoirs
of writing, writing that dreams.
Of puncture, of coming on its own.
Without choice. Without occasion
or even a subject. Without work.
Without responsibility.

The Lost Room

There was a room, I thought,
    under our kitchen.

I looked down into darkness
    when we came here,

caught stone crumbs blinking
    in my torch beam.

I looked down into darkness
    at black dice,

spent jewels, petrified milt, dust
    smoking itself,

and my heart clanged open,
    clanged right open,

—the bluebells are out in the wood!—
    and into itself

took one more lost note back.
    I sang that room,

the dream of opening a space,
    for a long time.

I sang not the knocking through
    and digging out:

I sang only the room ready
    to be breathed in.

I tuned and polished that dream
    for a long time

until I could see my steps
    work in it,

feel my voice bound in it.
    And if I said

that, in the dream of the room
    I sang, I saw,

I think, a possibility,
    two or three frames,

of being saved—if I said
    that, I'd agree

straight away it was asking
    for a hammer

too, but there *was* comfort
    in having work left

to do, an action I could see
    the end of,

in the hope of appointing
    this dream of myself

as myself—I can't say more
    or better.

I thought there was a room
    but it's a void.

My neighbour uncovered
    his and told me,

uncovered his and showed me,
    lifting a new board

he was about to nail down.
    When I told him

about my room I heard
    the Devil

sneering, sniggering;
    taking back

into himself one more bit
    of the world

that's his business; and leaving
    me one more lost note.

I heard the Devil laughing
    as the dream

of the room flickered and shrank
    to a dot,

a dot that floated off
    and was lost

in the dust that is all
    the lost bits,

the dust of the world
    smoking itself.

Winter Windows

i.m. Steve Lacy, musician, 1934—2004

"The winter begins
to strike gray here.
I think it's all the emptiness
that provokes the visions
(resolutions) that emerge
as the year turns,"
writes a West Coast friend,
rover of Mt. Tamalpais;
and the empty trees
crazing brittle light
do tempt one's thoughts
to ideograms,
things simple but full,
stick figures, letters
one looks *through*.

Close by but hidden,
struck metal measures,
unsentimentally,
how the day shrinks.
Kids' rhyme with a frost
love song left to rust,
—the only waltzes
for days of oil wanted,
of puzzle and crake,
traces in spaces.
Music with a twist
but the citric note
become the tune's
internal exile
from its own sugars;

become the way
to find the enormous
inside the tiny;
music like Lacy's.
As in: a workshop
on Monk's 'Friday the 13th'
devoted to
the stutter
in the second measure;
how most miss it out
and so miss Monk.
Monk doesn't miss them.
As in: a soprano
blown into the strings
of an upright piano,

its blowing away
listened to
intently,
each note's past
a question from the future.
As winter strikes,
this is what might come
to us down the ache
where sky was,
the haunt
of separate birds.
This is what comes
to me from seeing
you but never meeting you;
from knowing you only with my ears.

Now I think I'd like
to check some titles:
troubles, trickles,
clangs and clinkers,
gleam, blinks, the window.
Now I'll sing you
something for the season
with a dogged, dry lilt;
a slow-toying, paternoster work-out.
Something that plays off
closed and open,
as if a squawk
could blossom and fruit.
Something I learnt
meeting you in my ears.

Music is a way
to live small figures
repeated as if
you don't know how to
but have to
                music
is a way to live
as if breaths are steps
rising and falling
so time accents space
accents time
                music
is an endless stair
guesses where we go
where it winds and how

as if you don't know
but have to
                    music
is a way but not
not that line in Proust
that says the only
good paradises
are lost ones
                    music
is a way to live
now repeated now
as if you don't know
as if you don't know
now now slow forward

Near Death

in memory of Elisabeth Kübler-Ross 1926–2004 on Holocaust Day, 27.01.05

Winds crash into January,
whipping us through the cities,
working us hard through the grief
of short days and big red suns
blowing out and going down
the minute they catch fire.
Good you went out in August,
the season dressed in travellers.
One more winter would have been
a damn procrastination,
the gate closed, the plane waiting
but not moving, the work done.

It started in Maidanek:
on the walls of the barracks
were hundreds of butterflies.
On the walls of the barracks,
walls of nothing to hope for,
children already crossed off
all the lists of the living
scratched them, carved them, then left them,
the hundreds of butterflies.
It started in Maidanek:
all the butterflies speaking
from the walls of no answers.

Fast forward one decade, two:
all over the Western world
no-one was dying, no-one.
All through the Fifties, into
the Sixties, the doctors were
adamant: 'no dying here!'
You walked through the hospitals,
crossed arctics of loneliness
found the rooms of the dying,

the rooms of no answers.
You held out your tongue to them,
let their words fill up the world.

In your last years, after strokes
and a fire, as you waited
for what you called 'transition',
in changed times critics gathered.
Your five stages were too neat,
some said; were not even yours,

one said. So changed times change truth
into fashion, styles of will.
We no longer trust your kind:
accent thick as history,
charismatic, passionate,
unsentimental, stumbling
out of Europe's darkness,
blinking in the light you saved,
channelling tales of magic
and wonder. Enough! we cry,
away with your implicit
morals, reaffirmations

of faith. We only want to
watch reality and make
nothing better. So changed times
change truth, erase the moment
you grasped and, in grasping, made.
Back in nineteen sixty-nine
America was at war
with itself over its war.
It seemed the nation spewed death
and ate it, ate it, ate it.

The nation ate so much death,
denial wore itself out.

In a room, we remember
the dead with films, poetry.
We open our mouths, hold death
on our tongues in a plain room;
watch light's work on the clean walls.
A little way up the road,
traffic control deals planes up,
stacked planes down, drowns the squeals
of starting and the low drones
of ending in each other.
Winds crash around a plain room,
shriek through cracks, into our mouths.

The Waters

for whoever thirsts

I

Today I would be water:
standing, unblinking,
still enough to play back
every shiver of a passing
across and through me.
Today I would be water:
sweeping all before me,
muscling through gutters,
rattling windows.
Today I would be water.

II

A house of waters.
Of weeping and again weeping
and the washing of weeping.
Of cloths and basins and alabaster jars,
jars of ointment
and jars storing tears.
Of a slow line waiting
to write a name on a white stone
and leave it with the others.
A registry of waters.

III

What the sky wants
to form we don't know
but that it throws wind, drops rain,
and we are ourselves
suddenly, found pushing
into the air. This tear,
I don't know what it forms
but undwelling;
the water vase tipped over, cracked,
suddenly nameless.

IV

I stand in the road;
I hear the drains,
their ecstasies of rain
swelling the world's body.
A voice that is stopped,
subtracted, makes my tears.
I hope to move soon
through the clean air after rain,
freshened with birds singing.
I stand in the road.

V

Terry Riley on the radio
from L.A. as the sky gets black
with the rain they say will fall
heavily slash, stroke, oblique, virgule.
He says: a standpoint of supplication.
He says: whenever you're limited by something
you look more deeply into it
to find out what's there.
And so we look into ends
to know those who made them.

VI

What tears water—a date,
a distance—pitches us
wildly from wanting to
not wanting it fresh
and customary—which is some work.
But there is more, picked up
only when worked out;
something fresh but new:
one June morning, the pond
powering up a single yellow flag.

Three Postscripts

First Dream. The country is waiting for death. Everyone has become so convinced by the government of a forthcoming catastrophe, they've just given up on life. The colour goes out of their faces, paler and paler until finally white, and they walk out to meet death. For several days, the streets are crowded with people going out to find the forthcoming catastrophe and meet death. Then the city where I live is empty. I don't believe in the forthcoming catastrophe but now all the people have gone I can't find anyone who thinks the same way. So I travel to the city where I was born and where my mother still lives. My mother, I think, is one person I can count on to take a common sense view of the situation. On the way, I hitch a lift with a team of firemen. They are testing safety equipment so that everyone will be safe in the forthcoming catastrophe. The equipment they are testing turns out to be musical instruments kept in glass-fronted boxes at the roadside in the same way that defibrillators are kept in public places like railway stations. The instruments in question are like ancient lyres but bigger and bulkier and clearly electrically powered.

Second Dream. I am a journalist following the story of two software developers who are in dispute with Microsoft. Microsoft's new operating system keeps rejecting their program: it runs for a while and then crashes. Now it is crunch time: a meeting with Bill Gates. The meeting takes place in large informal lounge-like area. Gates enters with a large team of executives and lawyers in dark suits. He himself is dressed in a sand-coloured, beautifully cut jacket that is either suede or linen. He is surprisingly conciliatory and immediately starts talking about how the problem can be solved, customer confidence restored, etc. At which point, the two software developers interrupt him in order to present him with a gift—a musical instrument in kit form which they assemble for him. It turns out to be a weird hybrid of a classical lyre and an electric guitar. It emits a series of eerie high-pitched tones that are not particularly pleasant but strangely compelling. Gates excuses himself, gets up and leaves. After a minute, he returns, visibly angry.

He produces a pump action shotgun and shoots the two software developers and myself. We are thrown backwards by the blasts. After the initial shock, I realise I am not dead. I look at the stinging wound in my hand and see that we have been shot with cartridges loaded with rock salt like Uma Thurman's character in *Kill Bill Vol 2*.

Third Dream. Three coffins: jet black, shiny, closed. Three black coffins, large, medium, and small. Three black coffins, closed. Large, medium and small. Coming into the beach of a small bay. In that order. In desolate light. A crowd of people waiting. Many of them wearing cloaks and leggings and so conveying an impression that, despite the very modern-looking coffins, we are way back in the past, possibly even in Celtic times. The water completely still, silent glass, but the coffins moving. A mixed feeling attached to the scene, an uncertainty about whether this is a new arrival or a return.

Prospectus

Here to live differently
   for a while,
to feel the body work,
   time move.

Here to fit other descriptions
   of ourselves.
Whatever bit me yesterday
   called me 'meat'.

Here to live differently
   for a while,
to inspect the torque
   and mojo

of two snake vertebrae
   by a low wall,
to roll and be rolled
   over the edge

and bite of their casts
   of lost time,
perversely sensuous
   ur-forms

that keep making sense
   whichever way
you turn them over
   your fingers.

Here to live differently
   for a while,
to find what needs to
   happen happens.

Rue Longue Kitchen Song

In the kitchen
Jacques and Rhunette's

One bottle talked out
Another fetched

Setting the free world
To rights, its losses

And Jacques musing
On its bosses

Asks can you elegise
Those who aren't dead yet

The inverse of eulogy
Like a wish to forget

Out of the night,
Moths at the window

Sharing our light

Expressions of Eglise Saint Laurent

Watching the wEather
of liGht
alL day
tunIng
red tileS
ochrE black brown
and grey stoneS
up And down through
mIcro
toNes
perpeTual
Liquidations
Awakenings
and sUdden naps
giving the chuRch's
mEdleys
the differeNt speeds with which
They move

The squarE tower
liGht
rebuiLds it
x tImes a second
light iS always
looking whEre we're going
light getS to the future first
is somewhere we hAven't been yet
and lIght
Never fails
iT just gets beyond us
like the intervaLs
of chAnticleer's cocorico
just below Rue LongUe

cocoRico
perfEctly indignant
hunNdreds
of Times a day

we would neEd to know zero
his startinG point
just beLow the granite
cocorIco
percé Says a neighbour
commE un gruyère
to make sense of his silenceS
petanque tAnque petanque
an old camIon clangs
by below our wiNdow
The sun folds
its saiLs
and just hAngs
oUt
cocoRico
the villagE
spellbouNd
in lighT's subjunctives

Snake Folio: Two Scenes for Seven Speakers

SCENE ONE

A steep track: Trees sizzling
and hissing
in the hot pan
of the valley

A little dog: Dark spangles
of shattered air
under them

M. Frelon: The air is
a brass gong

First Stone: The big bang
of the Devil
laughing

Second Stone: The soil waits
to be glass

SCENE TWO

Mlle. Bigoudi, a cat: Somewhere close
as your pocket,
one tongue flick
approves this

A mummified rodent: commedia of dust

Second Stone: The valley waits
to be ash

First Stone: Snake starts what
snake will finish

La Spagna

Musica ficta,
adding accidentals,
        pauses awash

        with green noise,

tree static foaming
    in leaf shoals
        mocking the dry stream.

    The laptop drizzles
one passamezzo
        after another,

        tones of equal measure,

        over the dry stream,
    'some parts upon a ground',
            where stones in stones are drowned.

II

Musica vera,
crossing the stream, trudging
    round noon's turrets,

    all I see

here is being here,
    purged with heat,
        up by the old gate.

    Covenants of space
pull me through alleys,
        up steep cobbled paths,

        first one step then a half,

        above the old gate,
    to audits made in stone
            of settlement's full tones.

'La Spagna': dance tune for the lute, popular in the 16th century. *Musica
ficta* (lit. 'feigned music') is music in which the performer introduces
sharps and flats—often unnotated—to avoid unacceptable intervals.
Musica vera (lit. 'true music') refers to passages which involve no such
alterations.

Unstoppable Languages

Unstoppable languages
    took their energies

down the bypass
    and out of the valley,

says the empty café by the bridge,
    hanging over the Allier;

their way of having their way,
    say the ruins marked 'à vendre'.

The cadastre, parcelling land
    you either can't find or can't get to,

is a map of the commune
    only its ghosts could follow.

What got bounced out of the cart
    was people repeating

the same actions in the same place.
    What got left in the road

were explanations coming to an end
    in romances of the castle

overlooking hanging gardens
    where we see only matted *gradins*.

It's about as likely
    these woolly, windblown ledges

were where the serpent
    the centurion saint's killing in the church

would curl round the rock
    and sleep off midday.

Yes, explanations come to an end somewhere,
    and if weeds are flowers

in the wrong place then ruins
    are houses in the wrong time,

something that strangely pleases
    and upsets me every morning.

The Sounds

lien
the sound of the land
　　the soil in the soul
　　　　the twang
　　　　　　　Ustachon
　　　the First World War dead
　　　Biffe Plaix Vergezac
　　　　　Teyssèdre
　　　　　　　　crisp sounds
　　　　　　with a big beginning
　　　　　that's left in the air
　　　　　　　　hanging

La Charraira Longea

Where my steps enquire into
your quartzed tarmac tilt
and my eyes follow,
the world's abating inconclusively

into a dried, pressed frog, a rusting hinge,
a bucket with a hole in it,
scythe blades, file blades, without hilts,
and an axe head propped against a wall,

things forgetting their own names,
returning to the mineral.
A bucket with a hole in it isn't
anything except a sieve *brut*

or one that never woke up from nightmares
of being a short spout—and why not
'a memory like a bucket'? That would catch
the lifetime of unwieldy portage,

fighting the desire of the weight to get spilt
and lost, to jerk-tug-yank you left or right then over;
and, more vessel and process stuff,
a bucket's assumption of an urgent need.

Debris *would* lead to memory, wouldn't it?
Along this spare charraira, rare thoroughfare,
the urge to misunderstand, to just 'do loss' again,
script that lilt again, stitch one more thing into the quilt,

is strong, sighing through the old stone shells;
but vaults in the rock with their front walls gone
and houses with cleft floors and roofs of air
lay nothing to rest. They pierce us,

like light and weather run through them,
images of everything we are being inside
and this close to care withdrawn, being gutted,
unutterable—and we never can quite put that away.

'Charraira longea', phrase in Aranais, a dialect of Gascon, part of the
ancient Occitan group of languages. Literally, 'long street'. 'Charraira' is
also believed by some to have referred, more specifically, to a road cut into
the side of a cliff as in the subject of this poem.

From Brassac-les-Mines to *Le Vieil Auzon*

À sept heures du soir,
    above the high forest,
        eagles I think, big wings,

        others, mere scraps of birds,

    riding the reverse helter-skelter
    of the day's last thermals,
unravelling them,

        looser and looser,

    until one final twist
        pulls the birds out in stiff circles
            from which they pivot
                and plunge below the tree tops.

            Harald's place, just off the square
        all streets climb into,
    a sweet chestnut brandy for you;
'le whisky des français',

        a pastis, for me,

the day drifting off,
        not ready to eat yet,
    finding time to watch what water does

        falling into anise,

        the chemical marvel
    of glass turning opal,
eight o'clock rising.

Entry on Freedom

watching the air die
round marrows melons
acid loss already biting
the back of the trochee
anapaest amphibrach
iamb's throat damn
tree fizz
a subject for a poem
christine suggests knights templar
cleaning the cooker
or vegetables
she wears her laughter like a torch
the flies have it sussed
start out with a big idea
go straight for the sugar
laptop plays lute hits
from fifteen hundred something
wonder if anyone played air lute
behind us waterloo's garden of swords
armed men and women hiding their faces
as if looks could kill
aftershocks of four men
everyone asks after even here
when did freedom get so weak
it can be blown inside out
maybe we never had it
that's why loss is so big
you can't go free again
well 'let us remember nothing
but the days to come'
before back to being the filling

in a security / celebrity sandwich
spectacular poison
ah ah the noise that shakes the head
that says wait stop don't

ENGLAND–FRANCE–ENGLAND, AUGUST 2005

The Devil's Bookshop

for Jacques Terrasson and Jean Markale

I

Once upon a time, there was an English poet looking for a second-hand bookshop in a French village. He was down on his openings and almost out of beaten tracks until he turned down Hell Street and there it was and he came up Devil's Passage and there it was and he reached the end of Ginnel All Souls and there it was looking open and shut at the same time. So he went in.

The English poet had been into enough second-hand bookshops to know that they're rarely about books in any conventional sense. They often to seem to be walk-in display cabinets for all sorts of bizarre behaviours and goings-on. So the English poet wasn't at all surprised to find that the stock seemed to consist entirely of books about care and neglect. He wasn't even surprised to find that all the books he examined took the same perspective on care and neglect. They all described the ease with which people lose things or care about the wrong things or believe that caring about certain things is unnecessary or that not caring about certain things is the right thing to do.

The old devil who had the shop had a cunning motto written up on the wall. Sometimes it read 'J'aime mieux bouquiner que boucaner' and sometimes it read 'J'aime mieux boucaner que bouquiner' and he liked to try and catch people out by asking them what they thought it meant. The question of what things mean in a second-hand bookshop is always a vexed one. Meanings change depending on whether you're selling or buying or, according to some ancient and regional variations of the rules of the trade, trying not to sell anything at all.

'Bouquiner' means 'to browse old books' but is also common parlance for 'to read' while 'boucaner' is common parlance for 'to barbecue' which is a modern variant of its original meaning 'to smoke' or 'to cure' meat. So the old devil's motto could have meant simply either 'I would rather cook on a fire than leaf through a quire' or 'I would rather have my nose in a book than hang meat on a hook'. However, bearing in mind that [a] in *Roget's Thesaurus* 'cure' and 'smoke' are in Head 666; and, that [b] unlike a fool and his money, a devil and his fork are never parted, from the old devil's end—the end that wasn't his passage, that is—it was just as likely to mean 'A bird on the griddle's worth two in an idyll.'

II

Now, the English poet had had dinner the night before with an authority on all things Celtic and folkloric so he smelt an old goat right away. 'Bouc' or billy goat gets into the story because old stories used to be written on parchment made from goatskins. Indeed, an obsolete meaning of 'boucaner' is 'to hunt wild cattle or other animals for their skins'. It is also worth adding that another meaning is 'to worry, bother or scold'. The English poet knew all this and had noticed the motto changing each time he looked at it so when the old devil pointed to it and casually asked his question, he said without thinking "I would rather smoke an old goat than stroke an old quote and I'd rather turn a spit than pages of lit except on days when I would rather chew an old book than stew an old bouc or leaf through a missal than wear my teeth out on gristle and don't even get me started on *livre* and *chevre* . . ."

The English poet felt as if he could go on all day and, indeed, he did go on for some considerable time even allowing for time passing at a different rate in second-hand bookshops. He was still speaking when there was a clap of thunder. The devil gave a shriek and began to shrink followed by the shop and the English poet. Finally, there was an English poet and an old devil in some pages that looked open and shut at the same time waiting for someone to try and buy them from someone who was probably trying not to sell them.

Entry on Nation

there is isn't any 'version'
card nation stretched
but not allowed to break
fearful dream
in its simplest form
the attendance bonus is just that
our morphed hair shines surgically
deterritorialized
(a word that needs a line to itself haha)
infrastructure lures its photons
sing the portfolio clandestine
belt braces and parachutes approach bye bye
we got multichannel pipes
beating the target
'it's a mirror
you provide the formula'
psychically speaking
anything can be used to convert
sleep of desire to sleep of choice
and back then shuffle
so what you disguise in love with you
is what you see you get you see
and now the blues trouble and blether
where you are

SHEFFIELD, APRIL 2006

Mr. Fox
for Oz Hardwick

Once upon a time
I was in such a bad marriage with flux
sometimes my whole life seemed stuck
in a stopped train   stopped train   in the boondocks
outside some city   its sprawling sooty pomp   completely
    beyond me
and looking out from that stopped train's steamy box
I could see only a small part of my life and then not very well
just like you can only see a small part of whatever city you're in
the days were too long   the nights just a blink
I could have killed for a bit of equinox

I was getting further and further out of touch with flex
there was no room to stretch
in those stopped seats   stopped seats
my days seemed buried in their own ashes
before they'd even begun   choked from vox to socks
it was all a bit Pompeii
not the people baked in desperate supplication
more like those cooked off in their daily business
as if they hadn't noticed the sky thick with rocks

So stopped train   stopped seat   restricted view
except none of this had any weight
no avoirdupois   no troy   you'd need a mate to help lift
it was more an accumulation of flicks
rips and knocks   the body only feels later
well in those situations you take what you can get
that's how it went one morning
when the slow train did that funny thing it does outside Leeds
doubles back on itself   then deadlocks
and the sun zapped the train low and harsh

And at the corner of a field   the hedge was gapped
like a missing frame or an empty one
and into that gap   thrusting sharply
bold but not too bold
in a way that that made was so   and is so   the same so
into that gap   staring sharply
at the stopped train as if to say so what
as if to say stopped train and all of you stopped on it
are so far from being the centres you think you are

into that gap stepped
a fox

Entry on Noise

Summer hammers
and kids and dogs,
wind's wafts and mixes

of neighbours'
favourite chimes and tuckets.
Hoping for peace

in your own garden
is futile which I guess
is what you use

to roof a folly.
All noise simmers in
and boils over from

the larger politics
which, like the street tonight,
does everything with its mouth

and nothing with its eyes.
Something runs from here,
my 112th of an acre,

a string, a chain or a nerve
threading some beliefs,
interest payments, taxes

and votes I can't take back,
tying me in to
tremors, bombers.

SHEFFIELD, AUGUST 2006

[43]

Entry on Reading
for Andy Hirst

It's my own fault
   travels in the noise of text
war and barbarity
   protein degradation
nostalgic hierarchies cloaked
   in futurity or fantasy
savage kitchen stench
   of opinions and plots
doing the unspeakable
   to bodies presenting
the reality of bodies
   pushed here pulled there

Pulled here pushed there
   in the in the rush of head
cousin bard telling me
   anywhere is the heart
of the new plastic Europe
   a place to earn money
migrate receive influences
   to be cited sighted sited
as hits bits and dollars
   eyewitness journalist sub
information always behaves
   as if it were destroyed

As if it were destroyed
   travels in the noise of text
hits and reliability
   nonlinearities
Europe cloaking the reality
   of its unutterable new bodies
cut here thrust there
   in futurity or fantasy
don't assume the paper

[44]

in the language you don't speak
    isn't about you
brother skald laughing

My skald brother
    laughing another signal
perturbed it's my own fault
    voyeur of people reading
collective spectacular mourning
    more galactic prominences
too much information
    a joke simultaneously
bundling elegy
    entropy eulogy
the city's hot air rising
    makes its glitter flicker

SHEFFIELD–LEEDS–SHEFFIELD, OCTOBER 2006

```
          P
C H A N G E S
          G
for  C A G E
          S
```

Epigraph

What would you
make sure you took with you? $+ - \times \div$

found on a whiteboard, Leeds, 18.09.06

Prelude

Noises while Reading David Revill's biography of Cage
The Roaring Silence on the Bus, 11 October 2004

In the morning, the bus was unusually noisy. There was loud ambient sound as if a pink or white noise baffle was switched on. It quickly became apparent that the driver had forgotten to turn his microphone off. You could hear all his movements as he drove the bus. You could hear him breathing and cursing other drivers under his breath. You could hear air coming through a small gap in his window. Then a passenger asked him to turn his microphone off and you suddenly realised how noisy it had been compared to the usual morning journey noises.

In the evening, a young woman was studying a textbook about voice production. Over her shoulder, I read 'Silence occurs when no acoustic energy leaves the vocal tract'. A mad old woman sat next to her and started monologuing craziness at her. The young woman became more and more politely uncomfortable. I saw the young woman text a friend to ring her. When the friend rang, the young woman was 'absolutely impressed' so the friend must have guessed her predicament. When the old woman got off, the young woman started analyzing her monologue, its lack of pragmatics.

How to Begin

Water stops
at the proper time
and moves at the proper time.

K'AN — THE PERILOUS PIT

The Value of a Well

At first, I was disappointed with a well because I generally find that artesian 'depth' models of making art and poetry are irrelevant to my own practice.

Sometimes poems do seem to arrive from nowhere which may well be 'deep down inside' but, for all I know, is just as likely to be 'out there'.

But more often they come from reading and research and obsessive working and reworking of surfaces.

They come from words activating other words and sometimes from analyses and procedures that result in finding words inside other words.

So I was also disappointed with a well because it implies that you always know what you're going to get, i.e. water.

Then I read in James Legge's notes that 'the value of the well depends on the water being actually raised'.

He glosses this to the effect that the principles of good government are only good if they are actually carried out.

I'm not sure how much further that gets me but it made me pause.

CHING — A WELL

What is the Sound

what is the sound of displacement | unknown | but it is related to
the sound of governments turning away | what is the sound of
clouds forming | the sound of rain falling rain falling | plish |
governments turning away make weather |

KUAI — REMOVING CORRUPTION (BREAKTHOUGH)

Metallic Retiles / Fetlock Rebalance

I am thinking of Joan Retallack's essay in *John Cage: Composed in America* 'Poethics of a Complex Realism' and of the section titled 'Pothooks' where she says that every time she activated her Spell Check it kept suggesting 'pothooks' for 'poethics'. Pothooks are something you can hang your cauldron on.

Ting (The Cauldron) is only one of two hexagrams named from things used by man and both relate to nourishment. The other is Ching. To return to Retallack, for which my Spell Check suggests 'metallic', 'retiles', 'fetlock' and 'rebalance', she reminds us that Cage's life work was intimate with food and cooking.

I am thinking now how I love to shop for food and cook it but that I never write about it. This is new work for me to do after this work is done. But this is not only about me. There is more to say about food and cooking.

Choosing raw ingredients and cooking them is about developing attention and exercising it. It is also about bringing things out of potentiality into actuality. So teaching people about nutrition is not just about health. Pothooks are also written characters resembling pothooks in shape that are used in teaching people to write.

TING — THE CAULDRON

Radical Rest

From jawbones to toes: at rest. From cheeks to calves: at rest. And all in between: at rest. Rest becomes radical in a system that demands our production.

KEN — MOUNTAIN / ARRESTING DEVELOPMENT

The Scale

hospiTal visit
quicHe
madE in the morning

for Supper
reheated Carelessly
we both hAd food poisoning
three Levels
of carE

KU — ARRESTING DECAY

On Missing a Celebratory Lunch
through Food Poisoning

circuMstances
    nOurish
    yoU
    whaTever's
        Happening

I — NOURISHMENT

Something To Look At

this is a line and I
am breaking it
this is a line and I am not breaking it
this is also a line
that I am not breaking
and so is this

the hexagram for this page
has one line that
is broken and five that aren't broken
and this mixture of broken
lines and unbroken lines
looks like free verse

and so does cage's remark
in his juilliard lecture of
1952 about being in a state of confusion
where sounds are something to look at
the lines that are broken
are something to look at

TA YU — GREAT POSSESSION (ABUNDANCE)

I Eat My Old Virtue

I eat my old virtue
where I write from
a perfected suburb
or as close as you got once
till outskirts pushed further
and a made a new inner
till outskirts pushed further
and made outer inner

SUNG — CONFLICT

Off the Coast of the Poem

Off the coast of the poem
'don't trust journals'
well journals don't trust
none but the sick
would sail upon
what thou wilt not
and language
is a breeder
of the sworn
off the coast of the poem
'we often think of F_1
as the history of B_8
up to time t'
but most poetry
writes the inkxiety
of affluence
and fatigued
with nodding
'mmm, nice linch, ace'
I would mine eyes
discourse having some business
o as is the air
which gets us to
'I do not instruct
to annoy
the ignorant'
or 'And in the end
it meant so much
it really didn't mean
anything at all'
any which way
the trial's ache
earns starch

MENG — YOUTHFUL INEXPERIENCE (OBSCURITY)

Paint, Sauce, Self

on the 22nd day
of the work

there is the movement
of paint over wall

of sauce over raw dough
there are the words

towards away
the movement

of the self
between them

Pi — Union

We Speak

the first track
of the CD is called

'we speak'
but doesn't play

another explanation
on which I need not enter

T'AI — PEACE

Christmas Day Music

Take a cauldron that you can easily carry empty or full or partly full and whose sound when struck empty or full or partly full pleases you. If you do not have a cauldron then use a large saucepan that you can easily carry empty or full or partly full and whose sound when struck empty or full or partly full pleases you. Decide whether you wish the cauldron or saucepan empty or full or partly full. If you decide to fill or partly fill the cauldron or saucepan then what you use must be known only to you. When this operation is complete, walk through your district or town or city on Christmas morning with the cauldron or saucepan. When it pleases you or seems appropriate to do so, bang the cauldron or saucepan and shout, "I alone have decided what is in it and how much." Continue until you are so tired all you can do is sleep.

TING — THE CAULDRON

Some Error in the Text

There is some error in the text here
as all the critics acknowledge

is not a comforting thing to find
barely one eighth into a book of wisdom

men have used for centuries as an oracle
as a way of expanding consciousness

about the laws and rhythms of the universe
but post-WMD post Falluja

the future will hear
the tone of our age in the sentence

and anyway it will already have been written into
anything of importance so the judge

or the priest or the registrar will ask Do you
and the bride and the groom will answer I do

even though there is some error in the text here
as all the critics acknowledge

PI—UNION

Lie

haLf
prIce
salE

TA KUO — EXCESS

Thoughts Never Had

thoughts there are i've never had and never will how many have i
had so far how many will i have how is there a finite number at
which some well that's your lot mechanism kicks in how many have
i got left thoughts i've had same as anyone what is the ideal length
for a thought so many are forgotten but some have gone on for
centuries and caused a lot of trouble when does one end and
another begin what's the average number of thoughts in an hour a
day a lifetime is it different for men and women does it change with
age get better or worse if i just sat here and wrote down everything
that came into my head that would be a life's work if there was a
world record for thinking what would it be how would it work it
would be complicated for a start it would involve time and stamina
and endurance that would be the easy part then you could measure
electrical activity in the brain and look at it on scans there would
have to be agreed international standards on which parts of the
brain had to be active in order for contenders to even qualify none
of that would be too difficult but you still wouldn't have got down
to the business of the thoughts themselves that is how many
thoughts and of what quality that would involve believing what
contenders told you it would involve trusting them which would
be an interesting place to start

SUN — GENTLE PENETRATION

Shadow Haunted Movement

movement haunted by the shadow of this question that question is a bit of decoration around no

when i began this work i made a workbook to record the hexagram i threw for each day of making the work

i wrote two things on the cover at the top i wrote 'where would you go if you were going' which is from one of the stories cage tells in indeterminacy

at the bottom i wrote 'the world is too much rhythm' which is from my head as i walked in the district where i live on the first day of the work

this was to help remind me first that i was going and second that the work would discover attention or attend to discovery

or first that i was attention and second going

or first that i was going and second that no decoration bit question that question this shadow haunted movement

CHEN — THUNDER (EXCITING POWER)

Elegy

J i n g l e
p l O p
w H e e e
c l u N k

s q u e l C h
s c r A t c h
j a n G l e
E c h o

Note: The starting point for 'for CAGE: CHANGES / PAGES' is the *I Ching* in
the version edited and introduced by Raymond van Over for New American
Library (1971) which is based on James Legge's translation published in
1882. 'for CAGE: CHANGES / PAGES' was made during December 2004. The
sixty-four hexagrams were divided into four categories of work: free verse,
mesostic, noise and prose. Using coins, a hexagram was thrown on each
day of December. The number of the hexagram determined the type of work
to be written for that day. The contents of the hexagram—Judgement,
Commentary, The Great Symbolism, and The Lines plus Legge's Notes—
provided a starting point for each day's composition. A selection from the
daily compositions was made in late 2006.